NAPOLEON MEANS BUSINESS

I0467952

THE ART OF BUSINESS BASED ON THE MAXIMS OF NAPOLEON

By

STEPHEN F. KAUFMAN

Hanshi Warrior Press

Napoleon Means Business - The Art of Business based on the Maxims of Napoleon

Napoleon Bonaparte, war, maxims, business, strategy, tactics,

Kaufman, Stephen F, 1939 –

ISBN13   978-1500375096

Cover photo: Napoleon Crossing the Alps by Jacques-Louis David National Gallery of Victoria

Editorial Contact:
Hanshi Warrior Press
PO Box 135, Lenox Hill
New York, NY 10021
1-917-204-2670

First Edition and First Printing
1 3 5 7 9 10 8 6 4 2

for

Lita and Andrew

"Victory is the domain
of the most persistent."

NAPOLEON MEANS BUSINESS

THE ART OF BUSINESS BASED ON THE MAXIMS OF NAPOLEON

By

STEPHEN F. KAUFMAN

INTRODUCTION

There is no need to attempt an introduction of Napoleon Bonaparte; his contribution to the world and certainly to France is inestimable. He was, among many things, a major player in the structure of western civilization, and regardless of the final mistakes that he made, his influence is everlasting and, without doubt, quintessential in understanding warfare strategy based on desire and total conquest of the world in its own form.

In my previous books I have introduced a vast majority of the world to the works of Miyamoto Musashi's *Book of Five Rings*, Sun Tzu's *Art of War*, and the docu-fiction account of life in the court of Miyamoto Yoritomo in *The Shogun's Scroll*. Along with the precepts for understanding conquest in the Asian tradition, this present work will enable those biased for whatever reason to assimilate the same intelligence used in the world traditions of the West. There is no difference in application for the benefit of personal victory in any theater of conflict, including the business of business.

Napoleonic maxims illustrate in completeness and simplicity the knowledge that is required for winning in business situations where perhaps the ideal would be to compare business to warfare. I have chosen to use the parameters of business rather than martial conflict to alleviate the constant cloying and annoying barrage of death-dealing warfare that makes up the current ideology. The principles are the same, however, with the exception I have pointed out in my version of the *Book of Five Rings*: "There is a significant difference in not getting a deal signed and having your head cut off." Learn from Napoleon and recognize that my interpretations of these matters are lucid and extraordinarily functional.

Imagination is a requirement for intelligent and progressive management and leadership. Certain of Napoleon's maxims are very obviously military oriented but can be readily translated into a business scenario. You may or may not agree with the precept I propose, but the validity of the condition will always be realistic in regards to a commercial endeavor.

The fundamental ideas spoken of by Napoleon cannot be argued against. They are immutable and, as such, form an intrinsic aspect of study of any strategic complexity. I have chosen to incorporate certain ideas throughout this work in the expectation that although in business we are not speaking of killing in the physical sense, we are, however, thinking in terms of beating any form of competition. Do not concern yourself that some of the maxims are shorter or longer than others. Matters may take longer or shorter explanations and the intent is always apparent.

It is curious that a book eventually takes on a life of its own. What started out as a guide for business management based on the maxims of Napoleon can be a guide for maintaining visions of accomplishment in all aspects of life.

Stephen F. Kaufman
New York
2014

The Maxims

Maxim I: Campaigns of a military nature are generally beset with physical challenges that must be reckoned with such as mountains, rivers, deserts and cities. Each one has to be overcome at various times.

Business Commentary: In the course of doing business, regardless of the venue that must be approached, it is of considerable importance to realize exactly what and where you are moving towards and the reason for doing it. This consideration by itself will always tell you precisely what has to be addressed in terms of preparations and maintenance of resources. To accomplish your objective, all must be dealt with in like manner, such as the need to deal with possible limited resources, the heights to be scaled, and the torrents of rage that may accompany the passion of those involved with any conquest in any endeavor. Though there may be a hierarchy by definition, each one in its own place will represent specific problems that must be dealt with before additional progress can be made. It is necessary to know the "territory," or business climate prior to any irreversible decision is made.

Maxim II: When planning a campaign, the astute general must be aware of anything the enemy can and may do. He must prepare beforehand whatever may be required to counteract the possibility. Plans of a campaign may have to be changed in an ongoing process. The brilliance of the general must take into consideration the abilities of his soldiers and the obstacles to be overcome in the battle arena.

Business Commentary: In business, as with everything else that would be considered a valuable accomplishment, it is virtually impossible to understand and to become aware of every aspect of a campaign due to the frivolities of men. All known aspects must be carefully studied by managers, and the objective to be gained has to be understood by his most trusted staff. Once an operation is begun, it is essential that the leader be able to depend on the compliance of his people so that there is no series of surprises that can interfere with the accomplishment of the goal. Any time

11

an immediate plan is thwarted for any reason, there has to be an alternative plan at the ready to alleviate any form of total collapse of the intended outcome. It becomes more and more difficult to foresee a possible deterrent when the leader is not completely aware of the intentions of his working staff that includes sales, marketing and product development departments.

Maxim III: Undertaking the conquest of a country, a general needs to consider two aspects of the army: its vitality in neutral situations and in dealing with very great obstacles. Both aspects must be supported, or if one is left to fend for itself, both will become vulnerable.

Business Commentary: Managers and leaders can never assume that orders and directives are being followed in the manner that has been proscribed. Regardless of the sincerity of your associates and those under your direction, there will always be the desire of someone to usurp you, though their immediate intent may not even be obvious to themselves. Managers must be very astute in their hiring practices. If you are attempting to maneuver in two different directions, you should understand that each of the directions must be fully covered. Not to do so will only cause you to have to keep changing your focus until you eventually lose control of both.

Maxim IV: When more than one army is involved with a conquest, each will have separate lines of operation until all contingents are focused on one primary objective. This must be accomplished before the battle begins, and it should never be done in the vicinity of the enemy. This will enable the enemy to unite his forces, and knowing your intentions, readily beat your advances.

Business Commentary: When you are involved with the possible takeover of a situation that promises a potential for tremendous profit, you will generally need to have the cooperation of other parties to assist you in your endeavor. It is essential that all involved understand what the eventuality is expected to be, and each participant must understand their specific role in the venture. Under no circumstances should anything be discussed or developed where it is possible for the opposition to become privy to your intentions. The reason for this should be obvious, and there must never be trust where it is not required. If you are considering the applications of your endeavor as a long range situation, such as the takeover of a competitive corporation or business, why would you want input from those who are not in favor of your adventure? The rampant jealousy and loose-mouth tactics of those not in complete sympathy with your desires can seriously undermine your efforts. And remember, if someone is on your side today, they may not be there tomorrow. The only one you can trust is yourself.

Maxim V: Wars are governed by basic rules for victory. Every war must have a defined goal, and the basic rules must be observed. As well, wars should only be fought with adequate resources proportional to the obstacles to be overcome and the needs of the army.

Business Commentary: It is impossible to overcome an objection if you are unprepared to back up your situation with adequate resources and associates in alliance with your ideals. In business, where financial gain is a major aspect of management's focus, consideration of every participant's input must be realistically met. You must endeavor to maintain complete and total domination of the outcome in order to accomplish your goal. Do not expect others to be in accord with you if they have their own ideas about what should or should not be accomplished.

Maxim VI: It is most important to know when to advance and when not to advance. Once an assault has begun, it must be continued relentlessly until the objective is gained. Realize that there will be times when your most ardent efforts do not succeed, and you must call into action your alternative plans. The last thing to ever consider is retreat, which costs more in men and materials than the most bloody engagement and debilitates the morale of an army. In full combat there is the equality of loss by both sides when an impasse is not resolved. In retreat, the loss is primarily your own.

Business Commentary: If your plans are not clearly spelled out and understood by yourself, then how can you expect others to agree with your objectives? When you begin a campaign it is essential to continue on without hesitation to your goals and to have the resoluteness required for successful accomplishment. Be sure to understand what it is you want to accomplish, and trust in yourself that you will attract those sympathetic to your goals. If they indicate that they are changing their opinions, then they must immediately, and without consideration for their needs, be deposed and replaced where possible. If your desire is such that you will not relinquish your quest, then eventually you will gather around you those who will work to bring about your success. But, always be careful! Many people talk without substance other than for their own immediate gains.

Maxim VII: The army must be readily capable of resisting any incursions against them at any time. All equipment, armaments and weapons must be immediately available at all times. Each branch of the army must be able to support any other branch when required and be able to protect itself. When they are at rest, troops should be in comfortable positions and at the same time prepared for any sudden changes in battle conditions, possessing the essentials required for a field of battle. When an army is in marching mode, proper guards must be in place so as to forewarn the main force and in a position as to allow the main body to deploy.

Business Commentary: Your associates, and based on their complicity within the structure of your organization, should be ready and able to constantly reject any problems that do not coincide with your goals. All field and office personnel must have available all that is required for them to accomplish your means. Any time a new device becomes available that can be of benefit to the overall objective to be gained, these new tools must be provided. In this manner your staff and field people will always be able to communicate with the home office without being at a disadvantage when a serious concern arises. Your staff should be constantly on guard for such interference, and they should be readily provided with the comforts they need to enable them to maintain focus on the objective, which should always be the furtherance of your quest.

Maxim VIII: A new commander must constantly examine personal motives and strategies needed to maintain the advantage in a conflict. He must constantly ask himself what would be required if the enemy suddenly appeared in a place different from what is being prepared for. If this is not done, then the commander may find himself in a most disadvantageous position. Having to change strategy and tactics in the midst of battle will be very difficult.

Business Commentary: It is very important to keep yourself apprised of any eventuality that might pop up at the strangest of times. By keeping on top of matters at all times, you have the advantage of not being trapped by your own devices, especially when you are on the "march." And obviously, if there is any discomfort with the answers a business person gets from self-evaluation and situation events, an immediate change is required.

Maxim IX: An army's strength and fortitude can be measured by the quickness it responds to deployment and attack. As the army increases its velocity, the morale will increase proportionately. A road as clear of obstruction as is possible ensures this.

Business Commentary: When an objective has been defined, it is important that you insist on the compliance of all in attendance to proceed quickly and not let the opportunity get lost in the abyss of indecision. Your plans will be further disrupted if you do not maintain consistent focus on your objective. By not keeping the ultimate goal in front of your associates for them to be constantly made aware of, you will be further delayed from realizing your accomplishment.

Maxim X: There is no way to completely foresee events in warfare. There are times when the troops will be outmanned and outgunned. When this becomes evident, the wise commander will deploy the army with more rapidity to keep morale at a high level.

Business Commentary: The middle of a negotiation is not the time to find that inadequacies are prevalent in the overall negotiation. When those in your employ find that you are not preparing them with the correct equipment and information for them to fulfill their duties, they will eventually become disgruntled and be unwilling to work along with you. Always be prepared with an alternative plan should the necessity arise. This may sound redundant, but it is essential to the overall cause and must be repeated until it becomes a part of the consciousness of the entire operation.

Maxim XI: It is very difficult to maintain coordination between columns of soldiers when there is a separation because of a lack of communications. When attempting to breach a fortress and there are no direct communications for an advantageous maneuver, the outcome will be a continuation of breakdown in efforts. If one detachment does not know what another is doing, chaos can result. Time will be lost on the march and additional supplies may not be available when urgently needed. It is essential that all contingents be in alignment with each other to not permit the enemy to surround them or to pass them by. Every precaution should be taken to prevent an attack upon them when they are disjointed.

Business Commentary: Communications should not even be a requirement for discussion, but you would be very surprised to learn that in almost all instances that failed communications is the main reason for being unable to conclude a matter to your advantage.

It is imperative that communications pass from one member of the organization to another member of the organization, always making sure that it is never in the company of strangers. Do not let on what is happening in any aspect of your business dealings, unless those involved are required to know. Once your plans get out of your control, they will be readily acted upon by those not aligned with your ideas.

Maxim XII: An army should focus on only one goal of accomplishment. The idea of beating an enemy must be maintained as paramount with no let up in any area of victory. This attitude must be maintained throughout and not permitted to be diluted.

Business Commentary: Once you have set your plans into action, they should be completed as quickly as possible to prevent any mistakes due to misunderstanding of those in your employ. If they are not, you would find some among them who would seek to be creative without your consent. As well, you must continually reexamine your own purpose and be definitive in demonstrating your goals to all of your employees. This is another reason that proper selection of aides is of the ultimate importance and must be prudently monitored.

Maxim XIII: Distances that normally occur between different divisions of an army must be governed by the areas of conflict, sudden change in circumstance and by the objective sought after that should only change in dire extremity.

Business Commentary: Don't permit things to get out of control by not being able to communicate with your primaries as to what may or may not ensue as a result of your negotiations. Many times an astute manager will find roadblocks that were not perceived beforehand. This is a natural state of affairs in all negotiations, and it is essential that breakdowns not be permitted to occur due to a lack of understanding.

Maxim XIV: When in a geographical area that presents difficulty to traverse, the alert commander will always find areas that may seem easy to mount, but in reality are very dangerous to consider attacking, as they are usually deceptive when approached. It is important to maintain dual contingents that can immediately be used to support each other. When in this situation, it is required that the army be capable of forcing the enemy to withdraw, thereby causing the enemy to regroup at a disadvantageous time or forcing him to attack when unprepared due to your assault. With this in mind, it becomes necessary to maintain a guise of defensive maneuvers that will cause the enemy to attack and to do so on your terms.

Business Commentary: When there are more than two situations that must be dealt with simultaneously, it is essential that you understand the position and philosophy of each obstacle. It is not a good idea to try to have the marketing people intercede where a takeover has not been accomplished. The man of vision must be sure that each part of the team is watching each other's back. This is readily done by being aware of the many possibilities that might even stem from new business contacts being employed against you that you may have thought to be in line with your goals. It is always best to permit the situation to unfold in your favor by causing one of the opposing parties to make the first move based on your needs; therefore, throwing the others off balance by a deceptive move based on a renegotiation.

Maxim XV: It is essential that with all things considered in battle, that the glory and the flag be the first concern of a field proven general. The men under his command will rally to the cause and will acknowledge this and fight with more heart for an ideal higher than themselves. Their actions will result in more courage and conviction while they, themselves, will be more aware of their own camaraderie.

Business Commentary: It is important to understand why it is essential to negotiate for the benefit of all concerned rather than the simple seeking of personal advance. A leader who only thinks of personal aggrandizement will fall short of any lasting accomplishment. Those motivated for their own gain will always overlook the needs of everyone on the team. Though a powerful ego is a basic requirement for accomplishment, the overall ideal must be the first objective. To think otherwise will cause rifts in the team as individuals will attempt to do only what they think will hold them in good stead with management, much to the chagrin of the enterprise.

Maxim XVI: Never do what an enemy would want you to do regardless of how he may try to coerce you. The battlefield must have been previously studied, and you should know where he has placed his enforcements and armaments. This includes the principle of never attacking to the front if a flank action is better suited to winning the engagement.

Business Commentary: Having been successful in one operation does not always mean that you can continue to use the same strategy and tactics on a continuous basis. Once the "target" has experienced your ability, they can easily prepare to thwart any further attempt to utilize the same technique. In a negotiation, as with everything in life, there will always be the uncertainty of retaliation coming back at your best efforts with a resolved commitment to stave off your best efforts. Frustration usually accompanies the recognition of being overtaken. The objective itself, however, being dealt with by the opposition, must be guided along for the benefit of all concerned. Otherwise, continued petty annoyances will arise. The wise leader can sometimes use the same tactic twice, though certainly not a third time, except with the understanding of deception and perhaps a variance in the particular technique, thereby changing it, though ever so slightly.

Maxim XVII: When the army is on a march and preparing to enter into a combat, it is at its weakest. In order to maintain the proper formation and attitude necessary for victory, it is important that attacks against it are held to a minimum. When an encampment is properly handled, engagement with a superior force can be avoided if the troops are well fed and able to have the necessary rest by occupying a good defensive position. Poor entrenchment will not be adequate to protect itself by simply relying on a bivouac strategy.

Business Commentary: When preparing to meet with a negotiation team that may be more prepared than your own, it may be because of an oversight of your own team leaders, who did not adequately prepare for the process. When moving against an obviously more sourced confrontation or an inordinately financed contingent, extreme caution should be used prior to the attempt at closure. Extreme caution should be emphasized for all concerned on the approaching team, and they should have had good food and rest prior to the day's business. Should there be a general malaise brought about by lack of discipline and further preparation, then it would be assumed that leadership did not ensure success by proper study of the situation.

Maxim XVIII: Commanders and generals of ordinary skill, finding themselves in a precarious position and then attempting to deal with a superior force, will hardly be able to withstand an onslaught regardless of the courage shown by the troops. This can lead to a forced retreat, along with shame and dishonor. A prepared commander makes sure that all supplies required are available and does not hesitate to attack when the slightest advantage is determined. In this manner the suddenness of the approach can throw the enemy off balance, gain the advantage and maintain the honor or his own command.

Business Commentary: The primary mode of operation in any conflict is the conviction of superiority, physical ability notwithstanding, and the attitude of going into the attack. This mentality by itself will cause grave concern to a defending unit in the same manner as David and Goliath. The attitude of winning as the ultimate reason for negotiation is the main ingredient, and when the leader's mentality and attitude is in abundant supply, there will be resoluteness and cooperation without hesitation to get the job done.

Maxim XIX: Turning a defensive position into one of being offensive is a very delicate process, and much study of the pending conflict is essential.

Business Commentary: Turning the tide of a negotiation from one of potential defeat into one of absolute victory is based on the idea that the leader knows precisely what the intended goal is. When armed with this information and resolution, it would be most difficult for the opposition to ignore the propositions being presented by the advancing team, thereby forcing and subverting its own ideals to those of the business representatives at the table.

Maxim XX: The basic line of operation should never be abandoned, but should it be required to do so, it should be kept in mind that this is one of the most subtle maneuvers in war. A determined general must know how to change it when circumstances require it. When able to skillfully change the line of operation, the enemy easily becomes deceived and may lose control of where its primary forces are able to be deployed and what new points have become weakened.

Business Commentary: Once a leader has determined the direction of approach and close towards the intended goal, it is foolish to change course unless there is an urgent need to do so. Deception notwithstanding, any change that requires a significant revamping will cause utter delay and chaos to the line staff. It is best to employ deception when the leader's captains are unaware of the subtlety of the change.

Maxim XXI: When an army carries too many supplies and armaments and they are difficult to control the supply of, it slows down the entire army and additional consideration must be diverted from the enemy. As a result, the army can grind to a halt.

Business Commentary: It is never wise to overburden the front line staff with clutter that will slow them down and cause them to constantly ask for clarity prior to functioning. It affects their completion and gives them concern that the leadership is possibly unsure of itself as well.

Maxim XXII: It is equal to taking the line of battle that the army encampment is in position at all times to deal with any sudden changes in strategy and tactics. Heavy artillery must be in a functional place that can cover the surrounding territory as adequately as possible, and properly aligned sentries must be positioned to forewarn of any possible intrusions.

Business Commentary: In business, there is generally no need to camp out overnight in preparation for a "battle," but the same principle would apply when lodged in a hotel without the need for resources. Comparison can be made with the idea that whatever may be needed for a presentation is in place at the venue where it is to be deployed; advance hotel reservations should be in place; vouchers for meals must have been distributed, etc. It is also wise to have additional manpower at the ready to substitute in the event that a major player in your entourage is befallen.

Maxim XXIII: When the enemy army is encroaching on your position and they are apparently capable of overrunning you, without hesitation you must begin an offensive to thwart his advances that will cause him concern and make him change his plans.

Business Commentary: No doubt there will be times when you are unable to "breach the fortress." Even with extraordinary planning and presupposition, you may find yourself completely inadequate to the task at hand for any number of reasons. It is at this time that all your resources must be gathered together and a quick decision must be made to either continue or to pull back and further prepare. All of this must be done within the constraints of good timing and without the loss of face.

Maxim XXIV: Always establish your encampment at the furthest and best protected point from the enemy. This can be an invaluable position when considering the possible need to protect against surprise attacks. The additional time a general affords himself in this manner can be inestimable.

Business Commentary: In line with the thinking of Maxim XXIII, it makes sense to be in a position that cannot readily be overrun. In business, an approach can take on a variety of forms, including psychologically interfering with the opposition by your line staff.

Maxim XXV: When two armies are approaching the same objective and one must pass over a river via a bridge and the other has the ground to its advantage, it is generally observed that the ground force has an advantage, even if only based on maneuverability. A firmly committed commander must at that observation make a very aggressive move, strike forcefully, and outflank the enemy. Victory will be most assured.

Business Commentary: Should a situation develop where there are two groups in quest of the same goal, the astute leader will observe the manner in which the competition is approaching the target. Observing is not to be construed as permitting the other suitor to make an approach that would create an untenable situation. When the approach is observed, an immediate and resolute approach must be made, including the disruption of the other suitor in a most embarrassing manner.

Maxim XXVI: When communications are cut off between forces, it is essential to act separately and with conviction to obtain the objective. To maintain the thrust of the attacking stratagem is of primary importance and will bode a captain good graces upon success.

Business Commentary: In a negotiation situation, you are there to accede to your goals as the primary reason of any encounter. You are not there to make friends, though perhaps as an afterthought, but not during the acquisition process that can lead to victory or defeat. You are not there to learn about the opposition's golf handicap. You are there to destroy his possibility of winning in your stead and defeating your purpose.

Maxim XXVII: The nature of battle will sometimes require the necessity of retreating. Columns in retreat should always leave adequate protection to the rear to alleviate any significantly adverse actions by the pursuing army. It is generally devastating to be insufficiently protected, and all can readily be lost.

Business Commentary: In dire times when a retreat or a backing off is called for, it must be done with dignity. If it is not, then you would be hard pressed to make another presentation under the guise of the same respect. When leaving the area, do so under the pretext of some sort of "other" emergency and leave in your place trusted staff who can assuage the prospect that the "retreat" is valid. The intended target may not accept the excuse, but they will maintain an attitude of respect nonetheless. That is human nature, and you should always keep in mind that when dire circumstances are prevalent, even the most hardcore adversary will concede. The difference is that YOU should be more hardcore when the reapproach is made and with more successful results in attaining your goal. If not, why waste your time?

Maxim XXVIII: It is never wise to deploy an army during the night previous to a combat. Many changes can occur during that time, including an enemy retreat or possibly extreme reinforcements that could nullify your plans. Either way there will be a requirement to reconnoiter in order to deal with the changes.

Business Commentary: Timing is an essential strategy and its discipline must be studied. Once a conflict is entered and it is based on logical planning, there is no sense in changing your course without a dire emergency causing you to make that change. Fear, as well as a vision of success, plays an integral component of every action done offensively and defensively, but once you have determined the course of your action and you put your team in jeopardy for any reason, they may see this as weakness and will possibly lose their cooperation on your behalf.

Maxim XXIX: Once a decision is made to enter into combat, it must be done with your entire force available. Preparations are essential and it must constantly be thought about. Ensure that all contingents of your plan are well thought out, and in this manner you will be committed to overcoming any odds.

Business Commentary: Once you have made a decision to enter into negotiations of any type, you must do so with utter resolve by going straight to the heart of the matter.

Maxim XXX: Avoid surreptitious movements that are contrary to the objective at hand. For example, do not put artillery in a position of defending a retreat action when it should be put into position that will afford the greatest advantage against an attacking army.

Business Commentary: If you are watching for the proper time to make your move, do so when the outcome is most likely in your favor. Never assume that your goal is more susceptible than at any other time. When you become aware that the opposition is realigning their thoughts, you may find that you did not acknowledge certain possibilities prior to your advance. On the other hand, if you feel that the reinforcements are merely a show, then proceed with all due haste and take advantage of the opportunity.

Maxim XXXI: Once a decision is made to enter into battle, there should be no doubt in an astute general's mind that he will meet with great success. He should take every precaution to ensure his victory by realizing he may be encountering an enemy with much greater skill and experience. This should not be a deterrent. To think in any lesser terms would be to suggest to himself that he may not be able to deal effectively, and the result will be devastating.

Business Commentary: When you win in a negotiation, no explanation is necessary. When you lose for whatever reason, excuses will always abound and you may end up looking like an incompetent. Losing to yourself is one thing, but to your men is quite another, and you will be hard pressed to gain their respect back in like manner that existed before you lost it.

Maxim XXXII: An advanced guard should be instructed to give you the necessary information that can ensure your success. They must be able to tell you of the need for maneuvering and what manner in which to do so. An advanced guard should consist of picked troops and the general officers that can be trusted for their abilities and knowledge and should consist of light cavalry supported by a reserve of heavy cavalry and by battalions of infantry supported also by artillery. If they are not properly instructed and do not return with what you sent them for, it would be an embarrassment for you and result in your failure.

Business Commentary: When you are planning to move on a certain objective, it is best to consider all possibilities of deterrence before making an overt move towards the objective. Always use "feelers" to scout out the land prior to just barging into an unknown situation that could cause you difficulty when trying to make the "close." This is the equivalent of using spies to penetrate the opposition's stronghold. It is essential that your "feelers" or spies must be proven and trustworthy.

Maxim **XXXIII**: It is contrary to the rules of war to allow ranks or batteries of artillery to enter into a combat unless you have taken all actions to provide you with a successful deployment. In case of retreat, the excessive armaments will make hazard your movements and cause you additional embarrassment, and they will probably be lost in your haste. Armaments should be left in position under a sufficient escort until you are master of the opening.

Business Commentary: You should understand that when the actual approach toward your objective is underway, all of your anticipated actions should be well protected if the need to reformulate your plans become a necessity. You must provide for the safety and security of those in your trust. All of this must be taken into consideration prior to forcing your hand.

Maxim XXXIV: It should be laid down as a principle to never permit the enemy to penetrate your cordons, unless it is a plan of deception that will draw him into an inescapable snare.

Business Commentary: This must be understood as an obvious condition. Do not send in advance members of your organization unless they are prepared and well fortified with whatever is required for them to lay the initial groundwork for your success, even to to the extent of you having prepared a completely odd mode of approach. Deception must be done in a most convincing way or the result will be havoc.

Maxim XXXV: Bivouacs of the same army should always be formed so as to protect each other.

Business Commentary: When you are using two groups that consist of different skills, there should be strong communications between both of them should a variance in your plans develop. It would be foolhardy on your part to allow a need for a third group to intervene due to your lack of focus. Doing so will only cause you to lose control and will inevitably corrupt the intention of your strategy.

Maxim XXXVI: When the enemy's army is covered by a river upon which he holds several advantages, do not attack in front. This would divide your force and expose you to be turned. Approach the river in columns and in such a manner that the head column will be the only one the enemy can attack. Let your light troops occupy the bank, and when you have decided on the point of passage, rush upon it and fling across your bridge. Observe that the point of passage should be always at a distance from the leading column in order to deceive the enemy.

Business Commentary: When you approach an objective and you find that the intended target has protected all of the approaches, it may be necessary to come through the back door. It is important that your approaching actions cause concern in the enemy camp and force them to turn their attention elsewhere. The confusion will make them wonder where you are coming from, and at that very moment you enter from a place that they are not concerned about. It always works, but only when you are committed to the goal.

Maxim XXXVII: When preparations for crossing a river have been put in place, traversing the river can be made easily when the army is ready to move. If preparations are not advantageously positioned, it should be obvious that great difficulty will appear, especially if there is heavy fortification on the opposite bank, and the army and the bridge would be decimated by the fire of the enemy. The most skillful generals, when having discovered these fortifications, can bring their own army to the point of crossing in a circuitous manner and attack around the outer limits established by the enemy in the form of a semicircle.

Business Commentary: In this instance the ground to be covered must include proper planning and intelligent deployment. In preparation for a negotiation, and when you have the opportunity it is sensible to drain the target's resources without hesitation while simultaneously reinforcing your own supplies, enhancing them where possible. If a resource that is unquestionably important is not readily available, then it is wise to hold off your approach because without adequate resources, your attempts at closure will be less than satisfactory. An interesting concept to be considered in this situation where the waiting is not an agreeable condition is that the leader should employ deception, causing the target to deal with the appearance of an approachment. This is the concept of approach/no-approach, and it has to be studied until there is complete understanding on the part of your management team. Any forms of deception are acceptable if it demeans the target in a most subtle manner.

Maxim XXXVIII: Preventing an adversary from crossing a river when he is supplied with pontoons is hard to do. At the moment your general has determined the difficulty in opposing the enemy's maneuver, he must take measures to take an intermediary position between the places he defends and the places he wants to cover.

Business Commentary: Assumption based on incorrect information can cause complete failure and the attendant embarrassment. If you are unsure of your sources of information, it is best to wait until you have more lucid data that can alleviate any presumption in your decision. As a matter of fact, approaching an objective without the proper information is more foolhardy than approaching with limited resources.

Maxim XXXIX: In Philipsburg campaign of 1645, General Turenne was attacked with his army by a very superior force. With no bridge available to cross the Rhine, he took advantage of the ground between the river and his camp. This is a vital lesson for engineers that along with building fortresses, a space should always be left between both constructions where the army can reconnoiter without having to compromise its security. It is essential that all accommodations before wide rivers be built upon this fact. Otherwise, it will prove inefficient and ineffective in the protection of the possibility of a retreat.

Business Commentary: Regardless of any advance situation that is created for the action of approaching a commercial endeavor, middle management plays a crucial role. While creativity in the advancement of a cause – any cause – is essential, complete understanding of the pending actions should be clearly explained to and understood by middle management enabling it to carry out precisely the directives being issued from above. Though they may implement certain aspects of the project, middle management and staff should never be permitted to do the thinking of the executive and ownership visionaries. This causes chaos and will eventually turn into a free for all with no one being able to maintain order. Top leadership should express their desires without hesitation whenever confronted with a situation that is becoming difficult to manage. If compliance is not forthcoming, detractors should be and must be replaced.

Maxim XL: A fortress must be useful in both offensive and defensive warfare. When properly constructed they will be viable for retarding, weakening and harassing a potentially victorious enemy.

Business Commentary: Whenever possible create difficulties for the opposition. Should they attempt to alleviate a situation, they will be hard pressed to do so if they are constantly being harassed by seemingly petty annoyances.

Maxim XLI: There are only two ways of insuring a successful siege. The first is by beating the enemy's army out of its cover, thereby forcing it into a place of great obstacle, such as a chain of mountains or a large river. Having accomplished this, the army should position itself behind the obstacle until the trenches are completed and the place is taken. If it be desired to take the place in the presence of enemy-relieving fortifications and without the risk of battle, all material, equipment, ammunition and provisions required must be on hand for the presumed period of duration. It is judicious for generals to maintain the lines of control and immanent deployment so that the army will always be on the ready to battle an approaching enemy.

Business Commentary: It is best to be able to just walk in and take over a situation; however, that is not always the case. In that manner it would be of little difficulty to continue on with absorbing the profits and market position with a gentle, "Hi there, here we are." Something of this consequence would fall into the ridiculous concept of 'win-win,' which doesn't work. The more realistic approach would be to alleviate any inconvenience on your part by having all of your requirements and resources in place prior to your approach. In any event, proper planning and judicious forethought will prevent the necessity of having to go through the ramifications of establishing counter-insurgency factors.

Maxim XLII: A general has said that "the army should never wait for the enemy in the lines of defense, but rather go out and attack him." There is no way to be the absolute authority in war, and it is dangerous to await the enemy within the lines of his defense.

Business Commentary: Never assume that the object of your desire is going to comply with your request for submission. Depending on well thought out plans, it is essential that your approach be without hesitation and not depend on preparing for the advent of failure.

Maxim XLIII: Those who proscribe lines of defensive entrenchment can afford themselves an auxiliary defense that is never injurious, invariably useful or practically indispensable. The principles of field-fortification will always require improvement, and this singularly facet of the art of war has not made much progress since time immemorial. Even today it appears to be less than functional than it has in the past. Engineers should be trained to bring this aspect of their craft to perfection.

Business Commentary: Insist that your secondary staff understand the importance of speed and resolve in your decisions without them having to do extensive research into the matter after the fact. As a leader you must keep all of your people on the edge of advancement in all disciplines necessary for success in your venture, and this consists of offensive and defensive situations suggesting contingency plans at all times. You may delegate to others, but at the same time you must trust them to comply with your directives in the manner you want them carried out. Do not trust others to do your job. If you are going to permit that, then make your initial move and then bow out gracefully or not and leave the area of conflict. You will have lost.

Maxim XLIV: If the battle situation you find yourself in does not permit the deployment of a garrison to remain for the defense of the town you have taken, you must still ensure that you have destroyed all facilities that can aide the enemy in a reprisal. Take every means to leave the citadel indefensible.

Business Commentary: Once the initial take over has begun, it is essential to keep your staff on the ready to dissuade any form of market interference by the opposition. All of your staff must be in compliance with your goals. This cannot be repeated enough. If they are not, for any reason, regardless of what you may presume others would think of you, get rid of them immediately and replace them accordingly.

Maxim XLV: Fortifications can only protect an army for a limited time. After that time has elapsed and their defenses are down, they should be imposed upon to put aside their arms. Civilized societies all agree on this point to a greater or lesser degree that the governing force of that defense will capitulate. There are some who would be of the opinion that there should never be capitulation and that all remaining stores should be destroyed and that there should never be a surrender; use the cover of night to make a hasty retreat. If the enemy is unable to destroy all means of defense, the enemy general should do what is necessary to save his men.

Business Commentary: Regardless of the initial objective having been gained, the astute leader will begin to debrief his staff and associates so they can begin to concentrate more heartedly on the reason for the takeover in the first place. They should remain aware of the situation though they may be more relaxed in their attitudes of vigilance. If all plans have been followed and instructions carried out to the best capability of the staff, then there is no reason not to allay everyone's immediate fears. That way they can become more productive, and the profit will follow.

Maxim XLVI: It is always wise to grant an honorable capitulation to an enemy force that has made a vigorous showing in their actions than to risk a desperate attempt to maintain their territory.

Business Commentary: It is important to stop humiliating the overtaken once the overtaking is completed. A wise executive leader will always find, and generally in abundance, those of the vanquished more than willing to lend a hand for the benefit of all concerned in order for them to maintain their own status quo and keep their livelihoods intact. To completely humiliate and debase the 'enemy' is foolhardy and will eventually cause great harm to your endeavor through random acts of sabotage that you can never be fully aware of. When you have given refuge to some of the fallen you will find alliances that can certainly be of advantage to you; however, don't assume that everyone is sincere.

Maxim XLVII: Infantry, fusiliers, cavalry and artillery are weak on their own. Always enable them to be of assistance to each other in the event of a sudden onslaught.

Business Commentary: This is self-explanatory. Never put one group of your organization in a position of alleged superiority over any other. To do so will cause the entire project to collapse on your head. Keep managers in charge, of course, but never permit anyone to assume undue authority. YOU are the authority and you must strive to make that known.

Maxim XLVIII: The formation of columns must be maintained in two ranks due to the effectiveness of the variations of fire power in different echelons. The effectiveness of too may ranks can be uncertain and frequently dangerous to the positions in front. In composing the main force in two ranks, there should be a supporting line behind them, and reserves should be placed in the rear as additional support if and when necessary.

Business Commentary: It follows that when one group assumes authority for another, the under group will have reason for rebellion in the form on non-compliance with your directives and to do it with the appearance of agreement.

Maxim XLIX: It is not wise to mix different groups of battle skills together. There will be many inconveniences attendant to this practice. Each will essentially lose its effectiveness and substantive movements will become impeded. The energy that each would individually exhibit will become compromised and confusion will ensue. It is always best to have each cordon in a position of support allowing freedom of movement.

Business Commentary: You should not mix the interests of the tech support group with that of the sales group or the management group. To do so causes confusion when each is left to their own devices as to what is the priority for accomplishment and delivery of the objective. Each group should understand the need to cooperate with each other for the overall good of the endeavor and in that way ensure their own success and future value to the organization.

Maxim L: Cavalry charges are effective at the beginning, middle and end of a battle. Ensure that they always engage on the flanks of the forward infantry and certainly when they are in support of the forward contingents.

Business Commentary: The importance of any group within a large force is the result of leadership evaluating the need to utilize their talents at the appropriate time in the planned takeover. Not to do so will cause them to think they are not appreciated; therefore, they will not do the utmost to their capability when called upon.

Maxim LI: It is the responsibility of the cavalry to follow up the victory. They will also impede the beaten enemy from attempting retaliation.

Business Commentary: Whether one particular group in your organization is favored over another is irrelevant when the particulars of a contingency are to be dealt with. Reinforce those who are charged with the responsibility of maintaining the structure of dismemberment of the opposition in all areas of cooperation.

Maxim LII: Artillery will always take precedence over cavalry and more so the infantry. The cavalry charges and has no form of protection from the normal fighting force, depending primarily on the saber. The cavalry should never be without artillery, whether attacking or in position.

Business Commentary: When all groups within the organization are adequately supplied with whatever means are necessary for them to function, then the astute leader will not have to be concerned with their abilities other than the insurance of their training.

Maxim LIII: When in position or on the march, the largest part of the artillery should remain with the advancing forces and the rest should be in reserve. There must be adequate ammunition to complement double the amount required to maintain support for two battles.

Business Commentary: The most refined of equipment should be with the most elite of the organization's producers. In the advent of a surprise encounter, there must be adequate reserves and it should be allocated to those with definite need. It would be foolhardy to give the stable cleaners up to date machinery when the transportation sector is unable to start their cars.

Maxim LIV: Heavy guns would best serve the advancing forces when they are placed ahead of the main forces, thereby ensuring adequate protection for the infantry and cavalry without compromise. They should be in position to adequately protect all the flanks and have no impediments restricting their effectiveness.

Business Commentary: Always insist that your most able managers are in place where they can be seen and where they will act most effectively to encourage the output of the line staff while also creating concern for the opposing management.

Maxim LV: Never put your generals into situations of a stalemate if he has the possibility of garnering supplies and provisions of the enemy. He must be able to supply his troops with their wants and needs.

Business Commentary: Wise management and leadership will always see to it that their staff will be adequately supplied with what they need, especially if they have earned the rewards thereby. If this is not done, they will eventually display discontent and not see the reason for compliance and, most certainly, at an inconvenient time for the higher levels of management.

Maxim LVI: Good generals utilizing well-organized systems, employing proper instructions and maintaining severe discipline always ensure the stability of their troops for the cause in which they fight. A strong spirit of enthusiasm along with a love of country, national honor and zeal will work on their minds with advantage.

Business Commentary: The only bad thing to say about morale is that it may not exist, and the reason for that is based on the insipidity of higher management. Reward your best producers in front of everyone. Likewise, levy restriction when necessary only when you are prepared to reduce their authority.

Maxim LVII: If a nation is without a military system and limited resources, it will be difficult at best to raise an army.

Business Commentary: Without resources of men and materials, there is hardly any strength other than attitude to take over a considered organization. Trying to accomplish something without supplies is like marching a ragtag army and preparing to feed them on berries and field grass.

Maxim LVIII: Fortitude and privation under pressure is the sign of a soldier of merit. Their courage is secondary; it has always been so. Hardship and poverty is their best teacher.

Business Commentary: Management should never be overly generous, for this will suggest to your staff that they will have less to do for more. Always overload your best staff with more than they can handle and see to it that they delegate to those under their control the functionality of accomplishment for your ideals. Everyone must be kept busy at all times, even in the hours of repose.

Maxim LIX: Five tools are requisite for a soldier: his musket, ammunition, an entrenching tool, provisions and his knapsack for storage. This must be reduced to the smallest size appropriate.

Business Commentary: It is not wise to overburden the preliminary staff with equipment that can be delivered by the support staff. To do so will cause the object of approach to see you as slowing down the inevitability that you are trying to see through. Star attractions do not carry their own instruments or amplifiers. Proper management policies will see that what is needed is delivered where and when it is required for success of the endeavor.

Maxim LX: It is essential that soldiers be aware of and attached to their colors. This is best accomplished by showing respect to the old soldiers. As well, the older soldiers should have increases in pay depending on length of service. It is the height of insult to pay a veteran less that a raw recruit.

Business Commentary: This should be self-explanatory, and unlike current ideas that are rampant in industry and commerce of getting rid of the veteran employee in favor of a recruit so less expenditure is required, this is about as stupid and greedy as it can get.

Maxim LXI: Words of encouragement at the onset of battle are meaningless. It will not make young soldiers braver, and older soldiers will disregard them. When battle begins the only thing a soldier, young or old, thinks about is surviving the onslaught. Words of encouragement should be levied before the first shot is fired and they should alleviate any misunderstandings of the general's intentions. All orders should be in print and placed in positions of ease to read by all cadres involved in the pending action.

Business Commentary: Stern measures about the possible outcomes of situations will only cause the staff to become nervous and figure out ways to ignore the diatribes being offered on their behalf. Field operatives and their assistants are more interested in what they can look forward to after a corporate takeover that will be advantageous to their lives. In business we are not talking about camping out on a daily basis or being away from home for extended periods of time. When the day's work is done, the staff is to be expected to be free to do whatsoever they want to do, generally within the constraints of good taste. Contemporary business practices of progressive firms see to it that the working staff has all the amusement they need in order for intelligent outcomes to prevail.

Maxim LXII: Tents are objects of observation to the enemy's staff. They should only be used by high ranking officers for the purpose of clerical work when required, but they can send information to the enemy as to your numbers and the placement of your army. They afford information in regard to your numbers and the ground you occupy. A bivouacking army in two or three columns is only distinguishable by the smoke of the campfires and is virtually impossible to accurately count.

Business Commentary: When the 'show' is on the road, all participants in the aggregation should be housed next to each other in the event that instant communication is necessitated. Top management should not share rooms with under staff due to the possibility of sensitive information leaking out, though all the participants of the action in the scenario should be in the same 'hotel.' Today, communications is instantaneous via email and cell, but distance can still be an impediment, depending on the situation that is being approached. Keep your staff together ... and know where they are at all times.

Maxim LXIII: Information obtained from prisoners should be considered with due caution. It must be evaluated and its real value must be estimated. A foot soldier hardly sees anything beyond his company, and officers of mediocre rank can usually only give intelligence of some position and movement of his own command. The general should not depend on information gotten from prisoners, unless it agrees with reports previously received from his own advanced guards.

Business Commentary: Without doubt the opposition is going to try and deceive your best efforts when they determine that their demise may be imminent. Whatever reports you may have as a leader of a group, effort prior to the initial approach should be carefully regarded and only then should the new information be taken into consideration or disregarded. If there is radical departure from what is your expected norm, a curtail of engagement may be necessary until clarification is available.

Maxim LXIV: Nothing is so important in war as an undivided command. For this reason, when war is carried on against a single power, there should be only one army acting upon one base and conducted by one chief.

Business Commentary: Coalitions are nothing more than politically correct, depending on the situation at hand. It is detrimental to any organization to be headed by two chiefs. Favoritism will ensue at the least and, at the worst, no one will know what to do about anything. If you are in charge, then you are in charge. Period. Do not violate your own power by permitting others to make decisions for you. You cannot allow directives to be unanswered and thereby establish a scenario for the enterprise to be usurped by those who would pretend to the throne. This is not the same as delegating authority to someone for a specific aspect of the project and be sure to put everything in writing. Never leave anything to chance, especially presumptive interpretations of your command.

Maxim LXV: The only true wisdom in a general is determined courage. Consequences of uniformly attended, long discussions and councils of war will follow at all times, and they will almost always end up by the adoption of timidity, which in war is always the worst manner in which to proceed. To maintain favor and to protect their interests if they are not secure will always be the most timid.

Business Commentary: If at any time your vision is incorrectly defined by any of your staff, they should immediately be corrected. If they are unable to come to terms with your directives, replace them immediately without concern for their welfare. When men question the legitimacy of their leaders, they may also be plotting a coup. Be on your guard at all times to see in and through all of your associates and managers.

Maxim LXVI: An astute general must be able to judge specific arrangements, and it depends on him alone to overcome difficulties by his superior talents and skills.

Business Commentary: The reason a leader exists at all is to provide encouragement to himself for his own dreams to manifest. That the business leader selects others to work in conjunction with him must rely on prudent judgment. Finally, all responsibility lies with the visionary leader and any success is attributed to him alone … as is failure.

Maxim LXVII: Permitting generals and their officers to surrender their arms when complete victory is not assured is a dangerous thing, as it may be used as a ruse in anticipation of unknown forces coming to their aid. Incredible odds have been overtaken when the only way out was death, and it goes against the military intention of a conquering nation to permit a way out to the weak, cowardly and misguided intentions of the enemy. Great ambition requires great resolve, yet the more obstinate the resistance of an army, the greater the chances of success.

Business Commentary: It does not make sense to afford the vanquished under any situation full freedom equivalent to that of the conquering group. It is, however, a good idea to permit the vanquished to show allegiance to you by their actions in the furtherance of the cause that vanquished them in the first place. If they do not concur with this logical attitude on the part of the new leader, then they should simply not be permitted access to the new organization. If those in the company that you have overtaken are in accord with your estimations, then they should be permitted to provide the very services that you are seeking to utilize. When someone has put their well-being on the line to accomplish something in the name of the leadership, then they should be given first recognition. Period. Not to do so indicates a lack of resolve on the part of leadership to care for its own rather than those they think will increase their own wealth by fraud and deception.

Maxim LXVIII: Generals and overall security for a sovereignty will be afforded little security if they permit officers to surrender arms and position in the expectation of favorable conditions for their like. This action will always be counterproductive to the efforts of the army and dangerous to the nation they fight for and will put their own interests ahead of those of generals. Such conduct should cause them to be immediately deposed. Anyone giving such an order, and those who obey, should be deemed a coward.

Business Commentary: Where subversion arises in any form, it must be immediately quelled by any means necessary. Not stifling a belligerency will permit the cancerous activity to grow until the people rise up in utter disgust and shame (yes, shame) and seek to convert matters to a more overall functionality. Treason is a matter of utmost consideration, and do-gooders in this matter increase the tension that continues on, interfering with growth in the new corporate environment.

Maxim LXIX: The only honorable way to be taken as a prisoner of war is if usage of arms is restricted or entirely cut off from one's allies. There can be no other conditions that will permit honor being imposed.

Business Commentary: In business where the leader of the acquired organization has fallen for whatever reason, and it is always that leader's causality, an astute mentality of moving forward has to be part of his makeup, especially when he finds himself in an untenable position and all of his support has faltered. There is no shame in this; however, certain considerations may have been overlooked that could have prevented this problem. Nonetheless, the defeat must be taken in stride, examined for its eventuality, and the leader, redressing his own ideals, must begin anew unless he is totally vanquished. Adroit timing would be more appropriate, perhaps, and a stronger, powerful assault be made in retaliation. It is never time to drown yourself in the throes of defeat and whining.

Maxim LXX: A general's conduct in a conquered territory is always fraught with difficulty. If he is too harsh in his manner, he will inadvertently give rise to increased numbers of enemies. If he is too lenient, he will be hard pressed to alleviate abuse and non-compliance with his directives. He must know the manner in which propitious punishment and justness allays any forms of sedition and reprisal.

Business Commentary: It is essential that the leader taking over the operation of an acquired business be aware of the possible sabotage inherent with the outgoing personnel. Compliance may be taken for granted though one should be cordial toward the personnel of the acquired property while ensuring not to trust them in the slightest. Remember, you have destroyed their ego by beating their leaders at their own game and they will look for any opportunity to exact revenge. It is human nature whether you accept it as truth or not.

Maxim LXXI: Certain acts of sedition may be executed by a general who will do so with the knowledge of his conquered adversary if it is to his own advantage. There is no excuse for this, and any general who would exhibit such behavior and sell information to another for profit is guilty of the lowest of crimes and should be executed for treason.

Business Commentary: It is necessary to be aware of the motives of your higher and closest staff. Are you sure of their loyalty? If there is the slightest unsureness, you will possibly become subject to their whims and wiles. They may pledge devotion, but given the slightest chance of overthrowing you, they will, unless they are proven field warriors and not clerks. It is essential that you unburden yourself with this type of coward.

Maxim LXXII: A general must never hide his mistakes by blaming his superiors for faults if they are not in the immediate area of the military campaign. It follows that every general is directly responsible for the outcomes of campaigns and should always explain his reasons for non-compliance and to demand changes to plans when necessary. He must do whatever is required of him to essentially resign if the orders he has been given will lead to the possible downfall of his army. The same applies to being given a direct order that will cause capitulation regardless of the directive from a superior. If the superior is on the battlefield, the general must ask for clarification, and if that is not forthcoming, he should refuse to execute it. This takes extreme courage on the part of a general who understands more than the superior the causes of potential loss.

Business Commentary: It is a fundamental requirement that anyone with the authority to conduct any aspect of a campaign be up to date with the latest information about the intended action. When a subordinate receives plans and orders from higher ups, they should be carefully scrutinized to see if they are in alignment with the overall plan of operation. If something is amiss and the person in charge of the order sees it and does nothing to question the validity of it, it is as if that person were in conjunction with the enemy and is, therefore, responsible for the resulting chaos that will certainly ensue.

Maxim LXXIII: The first qualification in a general is to be able to maintain calmness in the impending campaign and be able to determine the situation to his advantage if possible. He must remain totally objective and not surrender to emotions regardless of good or bad intentions. He must consider all reports and information in proper perspective. The information he receives should not be permitted to take a place of fantasy in his mind but must maintain dispassionate thoughts that would otherwise affect sound judgment.

Business Commentary: If there is a problem with the emotional stability of someone assuming management responsibility and it is obvious, then that person must be replaced. Bad judgment will result and can be the cause of the failure of a negotiation. Actions will ensue that are based on personal bias and not for the overall causation of success of the endeavor. The intention of high leadership should be that those in position of the decision making function must be level headed and not react with superfluous frivolity. Regardless of their political associations, it is their responsibility of high leadership to remove such people from executive positions, as they are not functioning through a medium of sobriety.

Maxim LXXIV: The primary qualifications of leadership should distinguish an officer by his having a thorough knowledge of the area of conflict, being able to order definite actions and issuing orders that are readily understood by all subordinate staff in as few words as practical.

Business Commentary: It makes sense for a leader to necessarily understand the objectives of any campaign. It is essential that the leader understand the qualities of his superiors and the qualities of the staff that he is directing, as well as his staff in general. Having the prerequisite knowledge and information required to proceed, it is his responsibility to ensure that those under his immediate guidance are also capable of carrying out his orders without hesitation or delay. His directives must be given in the sparsest of words and with the utmost definition so that no misunderstanding ensues.

Maxim LXXV: All commanders of individual batteries should understand and be familiar with the general principles of all branches in service. The general-in-chief should be able to communicate adequately with all of his officers as to ensure a successful campaign. He should be in complete charge in his possession of all aspects of the army and the dispositions of his chief officers.

Business Commentary: In many instances, if those in secondary management positions fail to take to heart the actual requirements of the forward leading staff, there will be a tendency of the subordinate staff to become lax in their attitudes for corporate success. As an example, the person in charge of supply must be in constant communication with the managers of different groups involved in the enterprise without questioning those directives based on personal need and, perhaps, avarice. They must perform adequately so as to maintain an attitude of morale that can further the success of the endeavor.

Maxim LXXVI: A general at the head of the army must be able to accurately reconnoiter the troops and provide proper guidance that can be depended upon. He should be capable of utilizing spies to his advantage and have an understanding of the people that will be conquered. He must have adequate resources that will enable him to intelligently decipher information he receives and to be quick to answer any and all questions put to him by his superiors.

Business Commentary: Preparedness rules the day in every aspect of negotiation and normal living. When placed in charge of an operation, it is foolhardy not to completely immerse oneself in the matters at hand. To be in charge it is essential that everything related to the endeavor be first hand information and never based on hearsay. Working closely in conjunction with the many variances of a situation permits clear insight into matters that must be addressed. When this is accomplished there would be no need for guesswork when questioned by one's superiors.

Maxim LXXVII: Generals must be guided by their own experience. Generals that have expressed genius, such as the correct application of strategy and tactics of Frederick the Great, as well as Alexander, Hannibal and Caesar have always acted on these principles and can always be learned by studying the campaigns of these great men. They used the basic principles of keeping their forces intact and together, not leaving weak points unprotected and grasping quickly the importance or non-importance of reported and gathered information. When an enemy determines that the approaching general is astute in these matters, it will result in panic by the inspiration of terror. These are the principles that lead to victory, and the general's own army will be inspired to follow with fidelity and loyalty.

Business Commentary: Every great leader and world conqueror has studied most of those who came before. Profitting from their experiences, they were able to make sound decisions that essentially guaranteed their good fortune even in the event of reversals of chance. When reading the words of Napoleon, consider that he, himself, studied without letup in order to issue the most intelligent orders and directives. He was master of his own empire, and with the exception of his fall from grace that was brought about by his own arrogance, he certainly accomplished what he set out to do until that point. It is always best to consider the needs of history rather than the needs of personal aggrandizement.

Maxim LXXVIII: Continue to study the campaigns of the great generals and model yourself upon them. This is the only way of attaining to your own greatness and of truly learning the art of war. Personal genius will become an enlightenment and you will learn to reject all ideas to the contrary.

Business Commentary: This is essentially the same as the previous maxim, and Napoleon undoubtedly repeats himself for the express purpose of reiterating his own desire to succeed in the manufacture of his dreams. Wise managers should heed the advice given and design their persona as an imitation of the past masters until they, themselves, become their own individual.

Maxim LXXIX: A general's first duty is to determine the action required to surmount the objections to his efforts that the enemy can oppose him with. He then makes his decision and moves to overcome them.

Business Commentary: Fairly simple to understand is that the need for planning and preparation is unquestioned. Are all of your resources as the manager in charge of the negotiations in line with higher management's desire? Can the odds being faced be overcome with steadfast employ, or is it necessary to withhold decisive action until a more advantageous time? Regardless, it is incumbent upon the leader and person in charge of the operation, business or otherwise, to be grounded in the reality of the matter before beginning any form of negotiation.

Maxim LXXX: The art of war as applied to an advancing general is to beat the enemy without having to compromise himself. He must delay the enemy, causing him to take imprudent risks that will further thwart his attempts at success. Strategies and tactics are only the means to an end. The attacking general must use his troops, his cavalry and his artillery in the proper order to ensure victory. Devoted study is a requirement for the general if he is to accomplish his victory.

Business Commentary: In matters of war or commerce, it is always wise to cause the opposition to constantly restructure their own defenses and cause them to suffer delays in their actions. Various means are available to the astute manager such as sending incorrect information to those that have relationships with the group that you are attempting to take over. Advising the groups in concert with your opposition can and should be delivered with adroit methods of deception that can seem to emanate from the target of your approach.

Maxim LXXXI: It is hardly possible and certainly most difficult to find all of the qualities of a great general in one person. What should be sought is an exceptional man with a good balance of intelligence and ability tied together with splendid character and courage. If any of these are lacking in a person, the supreme commander must know of them and realize that if one trait is more dominant than any of the others, his general's accomplishments may interfere with the overall success of the endeavor, and this must be realized by the supreme commander.

Business Commentary: A well-rounded person is always conscious of his own strengths and weaknesses. It goes without saying that when someone in charge of an operation is intelligent and focused on the needs of the goal, his own encouragement will undoubtedly overcome any difficulty and succeed in the whole execution of words and deeds.

Maxim LXXXII: Great generals will always acknowledge their shortcomings. Continuity of inordinate success may be attributed to good fortune and chance, but regardless, they are always the result of study, calculation and innate genius.

Business Commentary: Again presented is the diatribe of preparedness in all aspects of the endeavor prior to advancing. What works in correspondence against an objection that is used a few times will by its own very nature become apparent to the opposition, and knowing this, the wise leader will put into place variations that will permit continued success as the opposition starts to assume the same approach as always will be used. This is to the disadvantage of those under consideration for takeover as they try to figure out the next move against them.

Maxim LXXXIII: When on the march and after victory, an astute general will never permit rest for either the conquerors or the conquered.

Business Commentary: When management sees that behaviors are changing in the tactics of opposition, it is incumbent upon the astute leader to increase the pressure without let up, and in that manner, maintain the intensity needed to have the ultimate objective take on the aspects of submission. The prevailing group must also maintain an attitude of constantly moving ahead until all desired is attained.

Maxim LXXXIV: When acting without a plan or the necessary resolve to win a battle, it will make no difference as to the strength of his because he will always be inferior to the enemy who has strength of character and is determined to win the battle. The general without such preparations will always have to be on the defensive and will make countless errors to overcome his own shortsightedness.

Business Commentary: Without sensibility to the overall objective of the operation, even the most clever of leaders will falter due to lack of continuity and eventually cause the tide to turn against him at the most inopportune time.

Maxim LXXXV: A general who is in charge of developing and maintaining battlements must be able to direct the construction of such and needs a practical mind as well as good judgment.

Business Commentary: Various disciplines are required for success in a joint venture, thereby ensuring that each person in charge of a specific function be on top of the requirements of the objective, including the ability to communicate with other line staff to ensure the the successful takeover.

Maxim LXXXVI: A general in command of a cavalry must have mastered the practicality of his army and know the value of utter victory never falling into the abyss of concern for the lives of enemies and must never trust to chance of luck.

Business Commentary: It is common sense to know when and how and where to institute an action that can prevent failure. Rhythm and timing are essential ingredients when crossing into areas previously thought unapproachable. Knowing the strategy attendant to the success of a campaign can effectively bring about results, and proceeding with due caution, have a mindset of uncompromising conviction. In this manner the concept of losing because of misaligned intentions is overwhelmed by the visions of attainment.

Maxim LXXXVII: Once a general has lost his power to the advances of the enemy, he will not have the power to effectively give more orders. Should he give those orders in misguided hope of turning conditions back into his favor, whoever obeys him is to be deemed a fool.

Business Commentary: It is essential for the leader of a campaign to be well aware of the possibility of failure along with the possibility of betrayal. When delegating authority to a second in command, it is required that the intention of the subordinate be thoroughly examined prior to action being permitted to be taken.

Maxim LXXXVIII: It is essential for the general to properly place his troops, such as the cavalry being with the advanced guard and ready to support any wing that may need assistance with each component being able to support the other.

Business Commentary: Support staff should always be in close proximity to the primary advancing management team. It must include technical staff when required as well as supply groups within the advance negotiating party.

Maxim LXXXIX: It is never wise to hold back one component of the army in the wish that they can be used at a different time. Their talents and genius must be at the ready at all times. To hold them in reserve is to have an inadequate idea as to the power of combined forces. All segments must be used in combination to ensure the overall success of the conflict.

Business Commentary: Never rely on only one specific team to be able to complete the entire objective by themselves. This is fool hardy and is equal to the idea of butchers and bakers being machinery maintainers.

Maxim XC: Order and formation of the entire attacking force is based on its impulsion to triumph. This includes the intelligent employment of reserves and resources.

Business Commentary: When making an approach in negotiations it is essential to always do so with utter conviction and constant focus on an outcome of a successful venture. It is necessary to demand speed and resoluteness from the back up teams when necessary to end the authority of the defending actions.

Maxim XCI: Components of the entire army, wherever they are stationed, should always be adequate to complete their mission. Manpower must be deployed in proper proportion to the area of their involvement.

Business Commentary: When seeking to divert the energy of an objection, make sure that there are adequate resources available to those who would permit you to claim victory.

Maxim XCII: In a military siege the general's skill and genius will show when a full thrust of fire power is placed in a single point that has been weakened by previous actions. The adroit commander will continuously fire with an overwhelming force of artillery and force the outcome to his own advantage.

Business Commentary: Once it is determined that an opening has been caused by the approach and close of a negotiation, the intensity of determination must be increased to bring the objective into submission. When the leader is assured that there are adequate resources, then by all means he should proceed with firm intensity to alleviate any form of defense and objections.

Maxim XCIII: The better trained the infantry is, the more it should be used with discretion with the support of good batteries. A good infantry is the backbone of an army, and care should be taken that it is not forced to fight beyond their abilities. This can result in the strength being weakened and can quickly cause demoralization leading to defeat. An enemy general with more skill and who is better at maneuvering against an enemy will turn the tide even though his forces are no match against the invading army. To wrongly use your army will cause you to suffer disaster.

Business Commentary: It is not always a good idea to rely on the elite of your team during a negotiation, especially if it becomes a long and dragged out situation in the opposition's arena. If sudden reinforcements appear, the elite may be hard pressed to keep their own offensive intact. Use the elite members of your team only when well aware of the many conditions that can come from hidden surprises if conditions will allow the opposition that strategy.

Maxim XCIV: A well provisioned army of good size, especially when reinforced by a fortress or natural barrier should make its camp unassailable by an army double in force.

Business Commentary: What is obvious here is that the area of negotiation is necessarily located in a position that does not permit an opposing group to surround and possibly overwhelm it. If your staff is in position to rest after an extended period of negotiations and they are constantly assailed, they will lose heart and begin to wonder why top management didn't have the foresight to provide them with adequate security.

Maxim XCV: A general should never lose sight of everything that will enable him to succeed in his endeavors. War is fraught with inconsistencies and errors in judgment regardless of circumstance. It is a mark of genius in a general that he be able to profit from an enemy's mistake or, for that matter, his own to utilize that genius and grasp the moment by knowing when and how to seize the opportunity.

Business Commentary: Regardless of how your plans are thought out, there is always the reality that the opposition has their own ideas of how to thwart an overpowering situation. A keen leader makes sure that even though his plans are well thought out and seemingly impossible to prevent from unfolding, the most absurd of circumstances can totally upset any idea of victory. That is why the great leaders, after having given adequate thought to their design, are always prepared with an alternative approach to make sure that victory is assured — most of the time.

Maxim XCVI: Keeping reserves on standby is a foolhardy method of command. A general must always use everyman at his disposal to ensure a firm victory. Doing so he will win with complete success, and with there being no more obstacles to overcome, he will insure his conquest and can then relax while maintaining a watchful eye at all times.

Business Commentary: Never keep reserves on ice, in a manner of speaking, for a celebration that may take place the day following a successful business outcome. There are any number of reasons for this, including the perception of those who did the negotiating and having to stand alongside those who only watched that can cause friction between employees on any level. More importantly, the loss of morale seeing that those that did nothing are being rewarded just for having been observers and are being treated as equals.

Maxim XCVII: Intelligent rules to follow include never having to require that a part of an army to fight a complete army that has already been successful.

Business Commentary: When management understands the conditions of a pending negotiation, it is essential to make sure that they are not facing an overwhelming force of superior management skills that have already routed your primary representatives. Though there is always the outside chance that the small contingent can succeed, depending upon freaks of environment, they will essentially be macerated.

Maxim XCVIII: Having laid siege to a certain place, a wise general that may have beaten an enemy by surprise and gained a time advantage should take further advantage by erecting lines of defensive position. This will afford him an improved condition, and he will have derived additional power in the overall condition of circumstances.

Business Commentary: When you have made inroads into the opposition's stronghold and they are in the midst of frustration and capitulation, a wise leader will take time to reinforce his own ideas of total victory. As well, he will establish an area that cannot be suddenly breached that can cause his own staff to be taken off guard if they become lax in their own vigil as they begin to take things for granted. This is a form of arrogance and does not mean that the attack is made lax, but rather that when the matter of accomplishment is coming into view, the time is right to maintain the pressure and firmly, with resolve, finish the negotiations most victoriously.

Maxim XCIX: The commander of an army prior to and during a battle is not in a position to try to think his way through. His only thoughts should be to defend the fortress to the last man and deserves death should he capitulate a moment before he has no choice but to do that.

Business Commentary: When approaching to make the final close of the encounter, it is best to continue on until there is concrete proof that no more resistance is to be found. By relinquishing control of the situation due to self-aggrandizement is cause for the control factor of the management group to replace the leader for lack of performance, regardless of appearances.

Maxim C: When an agreement to surrender is forced upon him by surrounding bodies and is required during a siege, and the conditions are firmly established by the enemy, a general who capitulates must do so with honor. To do otherwise is to further imperil his army and himself and is a dangerous act of cowardice.

Business Commentary: It is a meaningless gesture to forsake the reason for taking the reins in a negotiation by not committing completely all that is required for victory. If circumstances arise that make it seemingly impossible to attain victory on your own behalf, then it should be based on the idea that you did not plan properly and you did not fully commit to your own ideal. When putting the lives of those under your command in jeopardy and looking for ways out of the situation at the beginning of difficulties, it is a disgrace and is cause for your own demise.

Maxim CI: Warfare consists of offensive defense as well as defensive offense, regardless of the aim of the ideal sought after. It does not matter where the conflict takes place.

Business Commentary: In all aspects of confrontation, irrespective of the amount of planning and foresight, circumstances will generally always arise at the most inopportune time. A leader with acute perception knows this possibility exists and puts into the training of his support staff the need to understand the parameters of attack/no-attack that can assure the skills needed to act in either fashion.

Maxim CII: Understanding warfare requires the ability to turn and reconnoiter in the instant without allowing the different parts of the army to be separated.

Business Commentary: In matters of tactics it is always best to maintain a continuous approach and close mentality so that the entire team, advance and support, can be used as one thrusting motion without having to split resources to cover inadequacies discovered due to poor planning. In the event it is necessary to change course during a negotiation, it should be with the intention of completing the forward motion to subject the target into submission with even more vehemence.

Maxim CIII: Field fortifications are always useful and should not be considered detrimental once they are thoroughly understood.

Business Commentary: The obviousness of this idea is that without ceding any advantage to the opposition, the intrepid leader and executive will always be aware of the protective measures required for victory. This includes the proper materials needed to maintain the consistency of causing the demise of the opposition.

Maxim CIV: There must never be restrictions to the advancement of an army. Weather conditions notwithstanding, it can march anywhere and at anytime wherever the men can place their feet.

Business Commentary: Never fear to tread where devils seek shelter. When approaching the opposition, wise leadership sees that the team entering the negotiations are fit mentally, physically and emotionally in their determination to ascend to mastery of the day, along with the heart and actions of the leaders themselves.

Maxim CV: One particular aspect of a battleground should not be the determining factor that will cause a decision for combat. All circumstance conditions should be thoroughly thought through before a determination is made.

Business Commentary: Proper planning will always rule the day. When approaching an objective that for any reason did not permit the approaching management staff full access to conditions, it must be in the power of the leader to be able to instantly make alterations to the approach and close modality. This is called maturity of reason and will always appear to the astute leader when it is needed and without having to go into deep meditation.

Maxim CVI: Diversified marches are best avoided, but if they are necessary, they must be as short as possible and acted on with great speed.

Business Commentary: At any time in a campaign where it becomes obvious to the leader that a change in strategy is required and a decision is made to carry out a new directive, it must be acted upon instantly and without recourse to committee meetings to attempt to determine whether or not the change is good for the overall situation. If you are in charge, then you are in charge and should not have to discuss your intentions with those under your direction. High echelon management has apparently given you the go ahead to conduct matters in the manner you deem appropriate and thereby have put their trust in you to accomplish their goals, and you must behave and act accordingly.

Maxim CVII: Under no conditions should you permit your army to pillage, loot and rape unless you are seeking to disrupt your own intentions.

Business Commentary: In contemporary society, this directive and maxim would suggest a brutal take-over without regard for the people and conditions that are being met with. The exact opposite is true in that given the advantage to be inside the opposition's territory gives you the distinct advantage to sabotage their efforts before your actual attack. It is important to remember that you are not there to make friends, though subterfuge may be important at the moment. You are there to denigrate and incapacitate the opposition in such ways that they are unable to counter your advances. And, if you are not there for that reason, then why bother?

Maxim CVIII: Beware of flattery from enemies. A man of honor will not permit flattery at any time, especially from enemies. Perhaps, and only perhaps after all hostilities have ceased.

Business Commentary: Beware of false flattery prior to the onset of a campaign. Man's nature is to be impressed with his own self-importance, especially when his initial approach is considered detrimental to the opposition. Insincere flattery is the greatest insult of all to an astute leader, and it should be taken graciously and with cordiality while preparing for a quick and determined savage onslaught that will be difficult for the opposition to deal with. It should be obvious that flattery is offered due to their concern that they may not be able to thwart your advances.

Maxim CIX: Prisoners of war should be shown respect, especially if they have proven themselves in battle. They should be maintained with honor and generosity by the conquering army.

Business Commentary: With rare exception, employees of the opposition must not be debased in entirety. With careful debriefing they can be made into strong assets once you have captured their hearts and minds. Any sign of ambivalence on an opposer's part should be cause for them to be dismissed and to include any aspect of their influence that can impede your own progress and safety.

Maxim CX: A conquered territory should be governed by the conquering forces by moral integrity. Local officials must be taught the conqueror's methods of administration and they should be reminded that they are essentially hostages. They should also understand and be convinced that to cause difficulty will result in their death.

Business Commentary: Do not under any circumstances be lenient to misbehavior on the part of the conquered party. They must be taught that any infringement or lack of cooperation on their part will be cause for their termination, including the destruction of their family and financial security. They must be made to take oaths where it is deemed appropriate and in the form that is readily acceptable to them, and they must be made to understand that violation of their sincerity will be cause for their demise and that of their lines of influence.

Maxim CXI: The natural surroundings of a taken territory have greater influence, moreso than education or local mores on the character and demeanor of the conquering army.

Business Commentary: Circumstances of a physical nature that surround an advanced party that will be relocated to new areas should be considered from aspects that will also permit the new places to emulate to some degree the homeland from where they originally came from. There must be adequate recourse to visitation privileges as well as appropriate conditions for their families to live in harmony and prosperity.

Maxim CXII: Exemplary generals have done exemplary things by submitting to the natural principles of the art of war. Using innate or learned examples of the wisdom of those that came before them along with an understanding of ways and means, they have overcome tremendous odds in their quests for greatness. Through imitation of these superb masters of war can a man attain to his own greatness.

Business Commentary: Anyone who has accomplished anything of merit has had to experience tremendous moments of doubt and insecurity until they have risen to the magnitude of greatness that they have seen in the great builders that have preceded them. Constant devotion to one's ideal and continued study of the giants who have gone before can only reinforce a dreamer's vision. Following in the footsteps of those who have gone before consists of standing on their shoulders as well, affording the observer to see further.

Maxim CXIII: In the case of naval warfare tactics as well as those of the army, when the admiral gives the order to attack, each subordinate should commit with vehemence the necessary action to ensure success.

Business Commentary: When the directive is given to make the moves required to subdue the opposition, all factions of the approaching group must be ready to move instantly and without time for reflection on the motivation of the leader. If instant response is not carried out, then the leader has apparently made wrong choices for his support staff and will have to suffer the consequences.

Maxim CXIV: In general, land warfare costs more in lives than battles at sea. Land troops are constantly under pressure to continually fight, whereas sailors finish the work of a battle and can then seek repose. The sailor is never without sustenance and always has room for common comforts. His discomfort is never fraught with those of the land troops who are always under threat from hostile citizens, being poisoned and natural impediments.

Business Commentary: It should never be taken for granted that appearances will reveal the whole truth of a condition. In a business, when advancing ideas to the opposition about the value of being associated with those who desire the takeover, there should be solid backup for the application of ideas that would need reinforcement. Back up is not to be overlooked for their value in the development of a strategy and it must be understood that they are not subject to the same constraints as the management team directly involved with negotiations.

Maxim CXV: Generals and admirals, by the nature of their tasks, require different qualities. A general is born with certain qualities of genius and inspiration while an admiral develops by his own experience, and the sea is a specific area of conflict. An admiral readily sees his enemy, but a general never knows where the enemy stands. With armies, the slightest change in terrain can cause an incorrect assumption. At sea, for the most part, things are in plain sight. A major difficulty for a general is that he must tend to the needs of providing all things for his men; an admiral takes everything necessary along on his vessel.

Business Commentary: This true essence of leadership is based on individuals knowing their strengths and weaknesses. Leaders come in all shapes and sizes, and depending on the requirements of the negotiations being entered into, top management has the responsibility for getting the best person to fulfill the objective of winning the negotiation. When all matters are taken into consideration for the successful denouement of the campaign and plans are laid out and alternate strategies and tactics are studied, success will inevitably follow. When all considerations are considered and the goal is understood by all parties involved with the situation, victory should be an accepted fact before the conflict begins.

About the author

Stephen F. Kaufman is a world renowned martial arts master, an authority on management strategy, reality facilitation training and is the author of the best-selling interpretations of *Musashi's Book of Five Rings*, *Sun Tzu's Art of War*, *Lao Tzu's Living Tao*, *The Shogun Scrolls*, *The Sword in the Boardroom*, *Zen and the Art of Stick Fighting*, and the Hanshi David Mann action adventure novels: *The Hanshi of Central Park* and *The Hanshi in Brussels*. He has penned more than 37 books and short stories. His work is considered essential study for individuals and organizations interested in progressive management and motivation development that includes life enhancement skills.

Stephen F. Kaufman is the founder and author of *Self-Revealization Acceptance*™ - *Your Divine Right to Live in Joy and Freedom* and *Practicing Self-Revealization Acceptance* - *52 Weekly Ascensions to Empower Your Life*, the first, foremost, and original reality facilitation concept ever presented to the modern world, in 1993, and guaranteed to bring immediate and permanent results. For more information on the author, visit http://www.hanshi.com

Titles by Stephen F. Kaufman

The Way of Modern Warrior
The Shogun's Scroll
Musashi's Book of Five Rings
Sun Tzu's Art of War
Zen and the Art of Stick Fighting
Self-Revealization Acceptance –
                    An Introduction
Practicing Self-Revealization Acceptance
The Lady of the Rings
The Sword in the Boardroom
The Living Tao
Portraits of the Living Tao
The Hanshi of Central Park
The Hanshi in Brussels

HWP

Hanshi Warrior Press
"…words that matter"

Hanshi Warrior Press focuses on books of merit that convey works of realistic spiritual ascension, freedom of thought and innovation in the worlds of Universal philosophy, martial arts, life strategy, business management, motivation, and fiction.

www.ingramcontent.com/pod-product-compliance
Lightning Source LLC
Chambersburg PA
CBHW051313170526
45166CB00002B/530